Re

by Iain Gray

Lang**Syne**

PUBLISHING

WRITING *to* REMEMBER

Lang**Syne**

PUBLISHING

WRITING *to* REMEMBER

79 Main Street, Newtongrange,
Midlothian EH22 4NA
Tel: 0131 344 0414   Fax: 0845 075 6085
E-mail: info@lang-syne.co.uk
www.langsyneshop.co.uk

Design by Dorothy Meikle
Printed by Ricoh Print Scotland
© Lang Syne Publishers Ltd 2014

ISBN 978-1-85217-474-3

Reynolds

MOTTO:
I will defend my right
(and) By God's favour.

CREST:
A stag grazing on a mound
(and) A fox.

NAME variations include:
Renaud
Rennell
Rennels
Rennie
Reynalds
McRanald *(Gaelic)*
McRannald *(Gaelic)*
McRaynold *(Gaelic)*
McReynolds *(Gaelic)*

*The spirit of the clan means
much to thousands of people*

Chapter one:

The origins of the clan system

by Rennie McOwan

The original Scottish clans of the Highlands and the great families of the Lowlands and Borders were gatherings of families, relatives, allies and neighbours for mutual protection against rivals or invaders.

Scotland experienced invasion from the Vikings, the Romans and English armies from the south. The Norman invasion of what is now England also had an influence on land-holding in Scotland. Some of these invaders stayed on and in time became 'Scottish'.

The word clan derives from the Gaelic language term 'clann', meaning children, and it was first used many centuries ago as communities were formed around tribal lands in glens and mountain fastnesses.

The format of clans changed over the centuries, but at its best the chief and his family held the land on behalf of all, like trustees, and the ordinary clansmen and women believed they had a blood relationship with the founder of their clan.

There were two way duties and obligations. An inadequate chief could be deposed and replaced by someone of greater ability.

Clan people had an immense pride in race. Their relationship with the chief was like adult children to a father and they had a real dignity.

The concept of clanship is very old and a more feudal notion of authority gradually crept in.

Pictland, for instance, was divided into seven principalities ruled by feudal leaders who were the strongest and most charismatic leaders of their particular groups.

By the sixth century the 'British' kingdoms of Strathclyde, Lothian and Celtic Dalriada (Argyll) had emerged and Scotland, as one nation, began to take shape in the time of King Kenneth MacAlpin.

Some chiefs claimed descent from ancient kings which may not have been accurate in every case.

By the twelfth and thirteenth centuries the clans and families were more strongly brought under the central control of Scottish monarchs.

Lands were awarded and administered more and more under royal favour, yet the power of the area clan chiefs was still very great.

The long wars to ensure Scotland's

independence against the expansionist ideas of English monarchs extended the influence of some clans and reduced the lands of others.

Those who supported Scotland's greatest king, Robert the Bruce, were awarded the territories of the families who had opposed his claim to the Scottish throne.

In the Scottish Borders country – the notorious Debatable Lands – the great families built up a ferocious reputation for providing warlike men accustomed to raiding into England and occasionally fighting one another.

Chiefs had the power to dispense justice and to confiscate lands and clan warfare produced a society where martial virtues – courage, hardiness, tenacity – were greatly admired.

Gradually the relationship between the clans and the Crown became strained as Scottish monarchs became more orientated to life in the Lowlands and, on occasion, towards England.

The Highland clans spoke a different language, Gaelic, whereas the language of Lowland Scotland and the court was Scots and in more modern times, English.

Highlanders dressed differently, had different

customs, and their wild mountain land sometimes seemed almost foreign to people living in the Lowlands.

It must be emphasised that Gaelic culture was very rich and story-telling, poetry, piping, the clarsach (harp) and other music all flourished and were greatly respected.

Highland culture was different from other parts of Scotland but it was not inferior or less sophisticated.

Central Government, whether in London or Edinburgh, sometimes saw the Gaelic clans as a challenge to their authority and some sent expeditions into the Highlands and west to crush the power of the Lords of the Isles.

Nevertheless, when the eighteenth century Jacobite Risings came along the cause of the Stuarts was mainly supported by Highland clans.

The word Jacobite comes from the Latin for James – Jacobus. The Jacobites wanted to restore the exiled Stuarts to the throne of Britain.

The monarchies of Scotland and England became one in 1603 when King James VI of Scotland (1st of England) gained the English throne after Queen Elizabeth died.

The Union of Parliaments of Scotland and England, the Treaty of Union, took place in 1707.

Some Highland clans, of course, and Lowland families opposed the Jacobites and supported the incoming Hanoverians.

After the Jacobite cause finally went down at Culloden in 1746 a kind of ethnic cleansing took place. The power of the chiefs was curtailed. Tartan and the pipes were banned in law.

Many emigrated, some because they wanted to, some because they were evicted by force. In addition, many Highlanders left for the cities of the south to seek work.

Many of the clan lands became home to sheep and deer shooting estates.

But the warlike traditions of the clans and the great Lowland and Border families lived on, with their descendants fighting bravely for freedom in two world wars.

Remember the men from whence you came, says the Gaelic proverb, and to that could be added the role of many heroic women.

The spirit of the clan, of having roots, whether Highland or Lowland, means much to thousands of people.

*Clan warfare produced a society where courage
and tenacity were greatly admired*

Chapter two:

Kinsfolk of
the clansmen

A name with two main sources of origin, 'Reynolds' has been present on both British and Irish shores from the earliest times.

In Ireland, it derived as an Anglicisation of the Old Norse personal name Rognvald, or Raghnaill, and was found in the Gaelic-Irish form of *Mac Raghnaill*.

In the seventeenth century, there was a further influx of the name to the Emerald Isle through the harsh policy of Plantation – the settling of 'loyal' subjects on land previously deemed by those held to be 'rebellious' native Irish.

Meaning 'son of Reynold', the Reynolds surname also derives from the personal name Reynold, or Reginald – from the Old English Regenwald, which itself derives from Germanic sources denoting 'power' and 'rule', or 'ruler's councillor.'

As is common with what is often the extremely complex transmission of names across both

geographical and political boundaries, large numbers
of the name also settled on British shores in the wake
of the Norman Conquest of 1066.

Many of these Anglo-Normans later settled in
Scotland at the invitation of David I, who ruled from
1124 to 1153, and who had become enamoured with
Norman culture and lifestyle.

But bearers of the name had also found their
way to Scotland much earlier than this – in particular
to the ancient western kingdom of Dalriada.

At some point in the early sixth century A.D.
the western seaboard of Scotland was first settled by
colonists who had made the short journey by sea from
the north eastern tip of Ireland, led by Riada, or Rita,
and who established what would become the mighty
kingdom of Dalriada.

Known in Gaelic as *Dál Riata* – with *dál*
meaning 'portion' and *'riata'* indicating the person of
that name –its royal centre was established at Dunadd,
'the fort in the river', an Iron Age hillfort near present-
day Kilmartin, in Argyll and Bute.

Seat of the kings of Dalriada until the formation
of the kingdom of Alba, or Scotland, through the mid-
ninth century union of the kingdoms of Dalriada and
that of the Picts under Kenneth MacAlpin – Kenneth I

– Dunadd is now under the care of Historic Scotland as an Ancient Monument.

The site today is a major tourist attraction for its intricate stone carvings and a mysterious hollowed-out basin and footprint.

It is thought that the footprint and basin formed part of the enthronement ritual of the Dalriadan kings – with the monarch placing his foot in the hollowed-out footstep and symbolically stamping his right to the kingship.

It is not known with any accuracy at what date ancestors of today's bearers of the Reynolds name first became settled into the vibrant Celtic culture of Dalriada, but what is known with certainty is that by the early to mid-eleventh century they were firmly established in both the Kintyre and Keppoch areas.

This was through their close kinship with the MacDonalds, more properly known as Clan Donald.

So close is this kinship that, along with others who include bearers of the names of Dewar, Gibson, MacAusland, Mackinlay, Phillips, Watson and Weir, they are considered a sept, or sub-branch, of the clan.

As such, for centuries the history of the Reynolds is intertwined with that of Clan Donald – whose main branches include the MacDonalds of

Sleat, the MacDonalds of Glengarry and the MacDonalds of Clanranald.

Through this, bearers of the Reynolds name, particularly in its Gaelic forms that include McReynolds, shared in both Clan Donald's fortunes and misfortunes, while bearers of the name today who can trace a descent from the Western Highlands and Islands may well have a heady brew of both Norse and Celtic blood coursing through their veins.

This is through the mid-twelfth century Somerled, or Somhairle, whose name means 'summer wanderer' or 'summer sailor', and who carved out a vast west coast fiefdom that included the south isles from Bute to Ardnamurchan Point in addition to Kintyre, Argyll and Lorne.

Fiercely independent, he considered he owed allegiance to no man, not least to the King of Scots.

It was following the death of David I in 1153 that his grandson, Malcolm, succeeded to the throne as Malcolm IV.

He inherited a troubled kingdom torn apart by not only internecine warfare on the mainland but also by the threat of invasion from the north by Vikings, who sacked Aberdeen in the same year that he succeeded to the throne, and invasion from the west in the form of Somerled.

A powerful group of ambitious magnates, mainly centred in the Moray area in the northeast of Scotland, resolved to depose Malcolm, replacing him with their own puppet king, and were joined in this bold venture by Somerled, who was always eager to exploit any opportunity for warfare and plunder.

In 1157, a year after he defeated his wife's brother, Godfred, the King of Man, in a sea battle off Islay, in the Inner Hebrides, Somerled, described as "a well-tempered man, in body shapely, of a fierce piercing eye, of middle stature, and of quick discernment", seized control of the islands of Bute and Arran.

Control of these strategically important islands increased the threat he posed to the west coast mainland and Malcolm, rather naively, sought to resolve the problem by ordering Somerled to surrender his domains into the hands of the Crown, thereafter holding them as a mere vassal.

Somerled's answer was predictable. He assembled a 15,000 strong force of kinsmen and, embarking in a fleet of 164 swift galleys, sailed up the Firth of Clyde to sack the town of Glasgow in a blood-crazed orgy of arson, rape and plunder.

Malcolm's loyal magnate in the west, Walter Fitzalan, the High Steward, hastily assembled a rag-tag force of other loyal magnates and their retainers.

Somerled, eager to face the challenge, met the woefully inadequate royal army at Renfrew.

Accounts differ on what now actually transpired on that bitterly cold day of January 1st, 1164.

One account is that a fierce battle ensued and, as Somerled's battle-hardened Islesmen rapidly gained the upper hand over the royal forces, the tide of battle turned when Somerled received a mortal thrust from a spear.

Dismayed at the loss of their leader, the Islesmen's discipline broke down, and hundreds were slaughtered as they fled back to their galleys.

Walter Fitzalan had, against all the odds, achieved not only victory over a much superior force, but crushed the threat to the throne.

A rather less heroic account of the victory, however, is that the High Steward had realised he had no realistic hope of defeating Somerled in a set-piece battle and, accordingly, bribed Maurice MacNeill, Somerled's nephew, to murder his uncle.

MacNeill accomplished this treacherous deed by gaining admittance to Somerled's tent after his army had encamped at Renfrew and stabbed him through the heart, possibly while he slept.

One tradition is that when Walter Fitzalan and other nobles came in triumph to view Somerled's corpse, one of them kicked it.

MacNeill, stung by this insult to what had been a great warrior and disgusted at his own treachery, stabbed the noble through the heart and fled the scene.

Somerled's domains subsequently split up among his sons, and through this he is recognised as the progenitor, or founder, of the mighty MacDonald Lords of the Isles.

With their motto of *By sea, by land* and crest of an armoured hand holding a cross, they became masters of a sprawling fiefdom, controlling a strategic sea route between the north of Ireland and Scotland's western seaboard from their base at Dunyveg, on the south of Islay.

Chapter three:

On the field of battle

It was in appreciation of Clan Donald's loyal support of the great warrior king Robert the Bruce that he rewarded them by proclaiming that, in future battles, they would be given the honoured position of fighting on the right wing of the Scottish army.

This was in the exhausted aftermath of the battle of Bannockburn, fought in June of 1314, when a 20,000-strong English army under Edward II was defeated by a Scots army less than half this strength.

Ironically, it was a through a misguided sense of chivalry that the battle occurred in the first place.

By midsummer of 1313 the mighty fortress of Stirling Castle was occupied by an English garrison under the command of Sir Philip Mowbray.

Bruce's brother, Edward, agreed to a pledge by Mowbray that if the castle was not relieved by battle by midsummer of the following year, then he would surrender.

This made battle inevitable, and by June 23 of 1314 the two armies faced one another at Bannockburn, in sight of the castle.

It was on this day that Bruce slew the English knight Sir Henry de Bohun in single combat, but the battle proper was not fought until the following day, shortly after the rise of the midsummer sun.

The English cavalry launched a desperate but futile charge on the densely packed ranks of Scottish spearmen known as schiltrons.

By the time the sun had sank slowly in the west the English army had been totally routed, with Edward himself only narrowly managing to make his escape from the carnage of the battlefield.

Scotland's independence had been secured, to the glory of Bruce and his loyal army and at terrible cost to the English.

Nearly 200 years later, in September of 1513, Clan MacDonald and their Reynolds kinsfolk were led by Alexander MacDonald of Lochalsh at the disastrous battle of Flodden.

This was where an estimated 10,000, Scots including James IV, an archbishop, two bishops, eleven earls, fifteen barons and 300 knights were killed.

The Scottish monarch had embarked on the venture after Queen Anne of France, under the terms of the Auld Alliance between Scotland and her nation, appealed to him to 'break a lance' on her behalf and act as her chosen knight.

Crossing the border into England at the head of a 25,000-strong army that included 7,500 clansmen and their kinsmen, James engaged a 20,000-strong force commanded by the Earl of Surrey.

Despite their numerical superiority and bravery, however, the Scots proved no match for the skilled English artillery and superior military tactics of Surrey.

MacDonald of Lochalsh was one of the very few Scots nobles to survive the battle.

The MacDonalds and their Reynolds kinsfolk also proved loyal to the cause of the Royal House of Stuart, supporting it throughout the abortive Jacobite Risings of 1715 and 1745.

It was during the latter Rising that Jacobite hopes were dashed forever at the battle of Culloden, fought on Drummossie Moor, near Inverness, on April 16, 1746.

In what was the last major battle fought on British soil, hundreds of clansmen died on the battle-field while hundreds of others died later from their wounds and the brutal treatment of their Government captors.

While it was battle-axe and broadsword that

many of the Reynolds name fought with as kinsfolk of Clan Donald, it was with much more modern weapons that they accrued honours in later centuries.

No fewer than four bearers of the name have been recipients of the Victoria Cross (VC), the highest award for bravery in the face of enemy action for British and Commonwealth forces.

Born in 1827 in Edinburgh, William Reynolds was the first soldier of the rank of private to be awarded the honour.

He had been serving with the Scots Fusilier Guards during the Crimean War of 1853 to 1856 when, in September of 1854 at the battle of Alma he rallied his comrades around the Regimental Colours to successfully stave off an enemy assault.

Later promoted to the rank of colonel, he died in 1869, while his VC is now on display at the Guards Regimental Headquarters (Scots Guards RHQ), Wellington Barracks, Chelsea.

Portrayed by the actor Patrick Magee in the 1964 film *Zulu*, James Reynolds was an Irish recipient of the VC for his actions during the Zulu War at the battle of Rorke's Drift, in Natal, South Africa, on 22/23rd January of 1879.

Born in 1844 in Dún Laoghaire, Co. Dublin,

he had been a surgeon in the Army Medical
Department – forerunner of the Royal Army Medical
Corps – when he was awarded the VC for his
conspicuous bravery in not only attending the
wounded but also conveying ammunition to troops
defending his small hospital.

Also mentioned in his VC citation is his fox
terrier Dick – for his special attention not only to his
master but also to the wounded as they fell.

Reynolds, later promoted to Surgeon General,
died in 1912, while his VC is now on display at the
Army Medical Services Museum, Aldershot.

Two bearers of the Reynolds name were also
recipients of the VC during the carnage of the First
World War.

Born in 1882 in Clifton, Bristol, Douglas
Reynolds had been a captain in the 37th Battery,
Royal Field Artillery, when he performed the action
for which he received the VC.

It was in August of 1914 at Le Cateau,
France, that he was instrumental in the re-capture from
the enemy of two artillery pieces. Later promoted to
the rank of major, he died in February of 1916 from
wounds received in another action; his VC is now on
display at the Royal Artillery Museum, Woolwich.

With his VC now on display in the Royal Scots Museum, Edinburgh, Henry Reynolds was born in 1883 in Whilton, Northamptonshire.

He had been a captain in the 12th Battalion, The Royal Scots, when in September of 1917 near Frezenburg, Belgium, he was instrumental in the destruction of an enemy pill-box and the capture of a number of prisoners; he died in 1948.

From the battlefield to the world of politics, Albert Reynolds served as Taoiseach (Prime Minister) of the Republic of Ireland from 1992 until 1994.

Leader of the Fianna Fáil party during his tenure as Taoiseach, and born in 1932 in Roosky, Co. Roscommon, he also held a number of senior Government posts that included, from 1988 to 1991, Minister of Finance.

Chapter four:

On the world stage

Bearers of the Reynolds name have enjoyed, and continue to enjoy, success at an international level.

The daughter of a carpenter for the Southern and Pacific Railroad and of mixed Scots-Irish and English ancestry, **Debbie Reynolds** is the award-winning American actress born in 1923 in El Paso, Texas.

Her first role was in the 1950 film *Three Little Girls*, followed later that year with *Two Weeks With Love*, with which she had a major hit with the song *Aba Daba Honeymoon*.

But it was her first leading role, in the 1952 *Singin' in the Rain* that set her on the path to international stardom.

She enjoyed another musical hit with *Tammy*, from the 1957 T*ammy and the Bachelor*, while she received an Academy Award nomination for Best Actress for her role in the 1964 *The Unsinkable Molly Brown*.

Other honours include the National Board of Review Award for Best Supporting Actress in 1956 for her role in *The Catered Affair* and an Emmy Award for

Outstanding Guest Actress in a Comedy Series for her role in the television sitcom *Will and Grace*.

She is also the recipient of a Lifetime Achievement Award in Comedy and a star on the Hollywood Walk of Fame.

The veteran entertainer has a son and a daughter, the actress **Carrie Fisher**, from her first marriage to the singer Eddie Fisher, while her autobiography *Debbie: My Life*, was published in 1988.

Also with a star on the Hollywood Walk of Fame is the actor, comedian and director **Burt Reynolds**, born Burton Milo Reynolds in 1936 in Lansing, Michigan.

Best known for roles that include that of Bo 'Bandit' Darville in the 1967 *Smokey and the Bandit*, other notable film credits include the 1972 *Deliverance*, the 1997 *Boogie Nights*, for which he won a People's Choice Award, U.S.A. for Best Supporting Actor in a Film and the 1981 *The Cannonball Run*.

Married to the actress Scarlett Johansson from 2008 to 2011, **Ryan Reynolds** is the Canadian film and television actor who won the 2012 People's Choice Award for Favorite Superhero for his role in *Green Lantern*.

Born in Vancouver in 1976, his other film credits include the 2005 *The Amityville Horror* and the 2009 *X Men Origins: Wolverine*, while he is also known for his role from 1998 to 2001 of Michael Berger in the television sitcom *Two Guys and a Girl*.

A former U.S. Marine who saw action during the Vietnam War as a reporter for the service newspaper *The Windward Marine*, **James Reynolds** is the actor best known for his role in television series that include *Days of Our Lives* and *Generations*.

Born in 1946 in Oskaloosa, Kansas, he is also the recipient of an Emmy nomination for Outstanding Lead Actor in a Drama Series for his role in *Generations*.

Behind the camera lens, **William H. Reynolds** was the American film editor whose many screen credits include *The Sound of Music*, *The Godfather* and *The Sting* – winning an Academy Award for Best Film Editing for both *The Sound of Music* and *The Sting*.

Born in 1910 in Elmira, New York, he was the recipient six years before his death in 1997 of the Cinema Editors Career Achievement Award.

From film to the highly competitive world of sport, **Butch Reynolds** is the American former track and field athlete who held the record of 43.29 seconds from 1988 to 1999 for the 400-metres dash event.

Born in 1964 in Akron, Ohio, he was a silver medallist in the event at the 1988 Seoul Olympics and a gold medallist in the 4x400-metres relay.

Following an unsuccessful legal appeal against a two-year ban imposed for alleged illegal drug use, he returned to competitive athletics and became the 1993 World Indoor Champion in the 400-metres dash.

Sailing since the age of only four, **Mark Reynolds** is the American Star Class sailor and Olympic champion born in 1955 in San Diego, California.

His many wins include, along with crewman Magnus Liljedahl, a gold medal in the Star Class at the 2000 Olympics.

In American football, **James "Hacksaw" Reynolds**, born in 1947 in Cincinnati, is the American former fullbacker and linebacker who played for teams that include the Los Angeles Rams and, from 1981 to 1984, the San Francisco 49ers.

On the fields of European football, or soccer as it is known in North America, **Mark Reynolds** is the Scottish defender, born in 1987 in Motherwell,

Lanarkshire, who has played for teams that include Motherwell, Sheffield Wednesday and, from 2012, Aberdeen.

Bearers of the Reynolds name have also excelled in the highly creative world of art, most notably the great eighteenth century English painter **Sir Joshua Reynolds**.

Born in 1723 in Plympton, Devon, the renowned portrait painter was known for the 'Grand Style' in painting which 'idealised the imperfect.'

The son of a village schoolmaster and one of ten children, he had no formal art training but taught himself to paint through studying the works of great artists.

A founder and first president in 1768 of the Royal Academy and knighted for his services to art a year later, his many famous portraits include *Charles Lennox, 3rd Duke of Richmond*, *Lady Caroline Howard*, *Elizabeth, Lady Amherst* and *Admiral Hood*.

Forced into retirement after losing the sight of his left eye in 1789, he died three years later.

From art to science, **Osborne Reynolds**, born in Belfast in 1842 but moving shortly after his birth with his family to Dedham, Essex, became a pioneer of the study of fluid dynamics.

It was through his research into heat transfer between solids and fluids that major improvements were made possible in the design of condensers and boilers.

Appointed professor of engineering at Owens College, Manchester in 1868, elected a Fellow of the scientific think-tank the Royal Society and a recipient of its Gold Medal in 1888, he died in 1912.

A research astronomer from 1991 to 2004 for the European Space Research and Technology Centre in the Netherlands, **Alastair Reynolds** is the science fiction author born in 1966 in Barry, Wales.

Winner of the 2001 British Science Fiction Award for his novel *Chasm City* and the 2010 Sidewise Award for Alternative History for his short story *The Fixation*, he has also been nominated on three occasions for the Arthur C. Clarke Award.

A newspaper editor, explorer, lecturer, author and lawyer, Jeremiah N. Reynolds, better known as **J.N. Reynolds**, was best known in his lifetime for his advocacy of the 'hollow earth' theory.

This now scientifically discredited theory supposed that the Earth contained a substantial interior space.

A convert to the theory, propounded by John

Cleves Symmes, Reynolds joined the lecture tour circuit with him in 1824, continuing with the lectures when Symmes died.

It was only over time that he began to entertain doubts about the theory – one which is thought to heavily influenced Edgar Allan Poe's 1838 tale *The Narrative of Arthur Gordon Pym of Nantucket*.

Born in 1799 in Pennsylvania, he edited the *Spectator* newspaper in Wilmington, Ohio, for a time while in 1829 he outfitted an expedition to the South Pole in search of evidence for the hollow earth theory.

Sailing from New York, the crew mutinied at Valparaíso, Chile and set the hapless Reynolds and one of his companions ashore.

On his eventual return to New York he appears to have, perhaps understandably, turned his back on scientific expedition and studied law.

He died in 1858, having become a successful lawyer.

On a musical note, **Paul Reynolds**, born in 1962 in Liverpool, is the former lead guitarist and back-up singer with the band A Flock of Seagulls, whose hits throughout the 1980s include *(It's Not Me) Talking* and *I Ran (So Far Away)*.

Also in contemporary music, **Tim Reynolds**, born in 1957 in Wiesbaden Germany, the son of a U.S. serviceman, is the multi-instrumentalist who has enjoyed success as lead guitarist with the Dave Matthews Band and as a solo artist in his own right.

His *Kundalini Bridge* won a 2011 Grammy nomination for Best Rock Instrumental Performance.

One particularly enterprising bearer of the Reynolds name was Richard Joshua Reynolds, better known as **R.J. Reynolds** – the American business-man and founder of the R.J. Reynolds Tobacco Company.

Born in 1850 in Patrick County, Virginia, the son of a tobacco farmer, he sold his share in the family business and moved to Winston-Salem, North Carolina, and started his own tobacco company.

Renowned for his capacity for hard work and business acumen, he soon became the wealthiest person in North Carolina – but much more wealth accrued to him after 1913.

This was when, at a time when the vast majority of smokers rolled their own cigarettes, he developed and refined the packaged cigarette.

Blending various tobaccos to find a flavour that would appeal more to smokers than existing blends, he developed the Camel cigarette – so named because it used Turkish paper.

The product proved so successful that, within only a year, Reynolds had sold millions of packs of Camels; he died in 1918.